ACTIVATE YOUR ACTIVISM

I0142286

BY

ALEJANDRA 'ALLIE' STACK

ROYAL
AMBASSADOR

Royal Ambassador, LLC

Publishing Division

Atlanta, Georgia USA

Printed in the United States of America.

First Edition.

Layout & Design: Arthia Nixon and Royal Ambassador, LLC

Library of Congress Cataloging-in-Publication Data has been applied for.

ISBN 978-1-7349861-1-2

www.royalambassadormedia.com
www.alejandrastack.com
@alejandrastack

This book is dedicated to those who paved the way for me and to those who will eventually follow

- Allie, age 15

FOREWORD

As parents, we want our children to have the opportunities we didn't have, be better than we were, and achieve what we couldn't. Some of us end up with children who are not the ones they speak of generally in the parenting books, the ones who your parents may not be able to advise you how to parent, but we know from infancy that they are the changemakers, risk-takers, and voices of their generation.

Raising a child in an environment that you were not raised in comes with challenges, especially when it comes to racial disparities, different generational traumas, historical stories, and realizing that all the things that made you amazing, someone else can hate.

I learned many of these lessons during my time in a small town in rural Georgia. I also learned that as a Black divorced mother, who is aware of and still of my history and the ancestors who lived so that I might one day live, I had a mission to equip my child with the knowledge to be the best version of herself in a world that might not always accept her.

Disclaimer: I'm not a perfect parent and my child is not the perfect child. This book is a reflection of her personal experiences and her opinions, not an official manual. There were times when others could not understand our dynamic but still observed and judged wondering how we overcame so much together. I acknowledge that there was a village that helped at different points in order for me to help my child. That there are some who came for a season and others who are here for a lifetime. That no matter where we plan on going, we must understand our past.

This book is a proud moment. Partially because I know my child enjoys being vocal but not so much into writing, partially because it shows that the examples I set and lessons I taught her are being implemented before she is even old enough to drive, vote or be declared an adult.

I especially want to thank James Stocks, Jesse Strickland, and Corlis Hudson Long (also Ebony Inn) of the NAACP selflessly taught my child to fly in her purpose after I knew she was ready to spread her wings beyond the nest I provided for her. We are forever indebted to you and not a day goes by I don't think of how you took us in. This book is a testament of what you poured into my child as village elders, honorary grandparents and more. We can because of you.

Also to the late Michelle Lewis who reminded me to never dim our melanicity. I also want to thank the educators along the way like Deetra Poindexter of Change 4 Hope who introduced my child to HBCU's from ninth grade onward and created a program to introduce Black youth to entrepreneurs, inventors, fashion designers, equestrians, and others who look like them.

Dr. Sheva Quinn, thank you and you for that final push by having Allie be a presenter of your Black Lives Matter course through your Black Classical University which allowed her to inspire youth. Janel Bailey Jones, thank you for challenging me to parent on my terms and to embrace the gifts she has in this realm.

Also, thank you to the iconic, Clara McClaughlin of The Florida Star for that spark you lit during the Gullah Geechee festival on Sapelo Island where you spotted the curiosity and encouraged Allie to tell the stories, further pushing her by giving her a trivia game on African-American history so that she at six, could have an understanding and appreciation.

The thing is, we can do what many did before us and ask our children to sit still and be seen and not heard. We can watch them leave for school, know they are with friends in malls, driving along enjoying music, and realize to someone, they are a threat based on their look, their complexion, or accent. We can ignore what is going on daily in the news or we can have the hard conversations, show them the research, let them hear from us directly, and prepare them for the situations they might encounter when we are not present.

We can show them the animals suffering, the environment decaying, the inequalities amongst people, or whatever they are passionate enough to activate their activism towards, and encourage them to seek out the information with our guidance. If they are old enough to attend events, tell them the correct ways to make it count. If they are too young to go in person, show them that their voice matters even if it is as simple as creating a poster and taking photos.

We are the educators of tomorrow's generation. We must not take that task lightly.

Allie, I can't put in words what I have seen in you these past 15 years. I will say that I am truly honored to know that I was chosen to be a part of your life, especially as the vessel to bring your forth. I am proud that you had the courage to share your passion with me. The trials and tribulations we have endured. The arguments I had to endure with others trying to explain that this was you doing you rather than me forcing you. 'Cause the truth is, you're kinda built for this far better than I think I am, Sis ;) Continue to stir up good trouble, to shift the conversation, to not only say that something would be a good idea but to actually research so that you can participate in doing something. May you rise and reign like the royalty you are.

Arthia Nixon
Award-winning journalist & Bestselling author
#PROUDMOM

ACTIVATE YOUR ACTIVISM

"Black. Hispanic. Immigrant.
Award-winning Journalist.
NAACP Youth Council President.
Youth Activist. Kid.
This is ME."

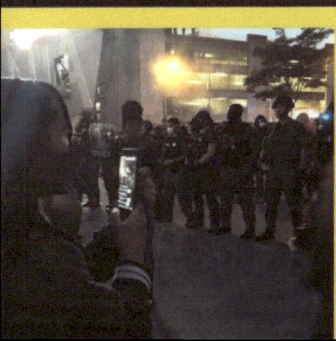

STORY & PHOTOS BY
ALEJANDRA STACK
FOREWORD BY ARTHIA NIXON

InDaHouseMedia "JEROME DORN"

Kidz Rock Awards

Journalist of the Year

Alejandra Stack

July 29, 2017

My name is Alejandra Stack, but I'm better known as Allie in Action or KidNewsMaker. I prefer to be called Allie.

At eleven-years-old, I officially followed my mom's footsteps by becoming a journalist and created a magazine called, KidNewsMaker. Because of that publication and website, I got to meet amazing people and win some amazing awards. That's another story for another day. This story is about how I became an activist.

I spent my early childhood in the Caribbean and while there, I remember seeing at least 90% of the people looking similar to me. I saw people like me on dollar bills. I saw women of African and Indian heritage as Prime Ministers and Governor-Generals leading countries before Barack Obama became President of the USA. My schoolbooks had histories of Amerindians and Black Caribbean people. I learned to love the skin I was in and didn't have to choose if I were more Black or Hispanic because I was taught to embrace myself. However, when I moved to the USA, some things changed.

I was still in elementary school when Trayvon Martin, a Black teenager from Florida was killed. I didn't understand why people protested in the wake of his death or why people were so angry after another teenager in Missouri, Michael Brown was killed by police officers. When I asked my teachers at school about it, I was told the school was not an appropriate place to talk about it. When we talked about Christopher Columbus landing in America, I corrected my teacher explaining that he landed on an island that used to be called Guanahani and explained the Arawaks, Caribs, Tainos and Lucayans, things I was taught by my mom and was a part of what I learned in the Caribbean. I was told not to discuss it in school.

So for a long time, I was quiet.

When my mom got a job as a reporter outside of Atlanta, Georgia and I was in a school of majority White students, I began to experience an identity crisis because to some of them, I wasn't Black enough, I wasn't Hispanic enough, and as someone whose mom had an accent, I wasn't American enough.

There was some good and bad in the new town, but one of the things that was good was when my mom took me along with her to cover a local National Association for the Advancement of Colored People event. I learned that the organization started in 1909 to stop racial discrimination. It's one of the most well-known organizations in the USA.

Because of the NAACP, I learned about a lot of things like peaceful protesting, civil rights, how to be a changemaker and I learned about many people in history who took a stand to

ensure equal rights, and to not live hating people simply because of their race. I also learned that there were many community activities to get involved in to use my time wisely.

I met with the local president and began attending meetings and became an official member of the NAACP at age 11. I joined the NAACP Youth Council and learned about other kids who were a part of the movement for civil rights. Kids like Ruby Bridges, who was just six

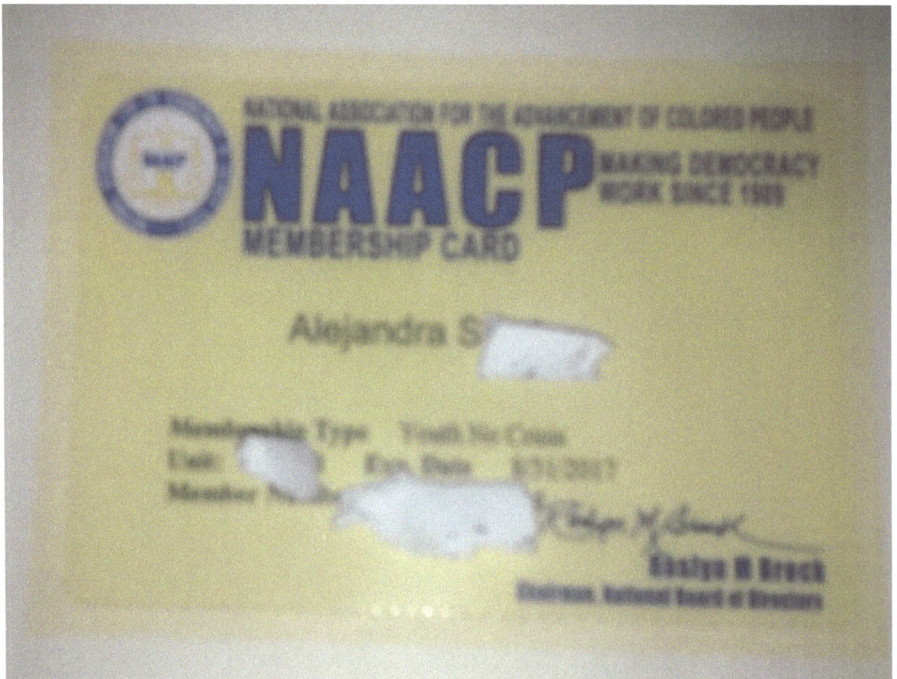

Martin Luther King Jr. Day Parade

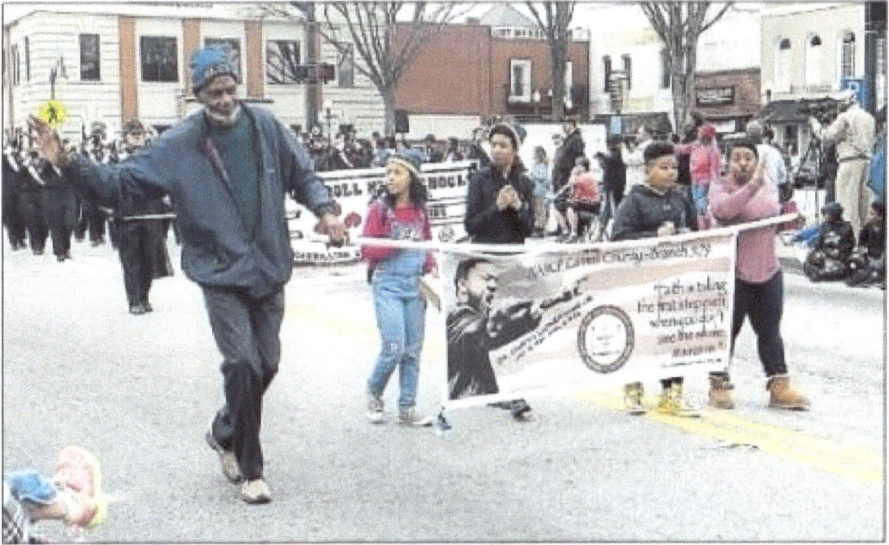

-years-old in 1960 when she became the first Black child to attend a White school in the South.

I thought about all the racial injustices that were still happening on the news all these decades later and wondered how I could get more involved.

Eventually, I was elected President of The NAACP Youth Council for my area. I attended events and marched in parades too.

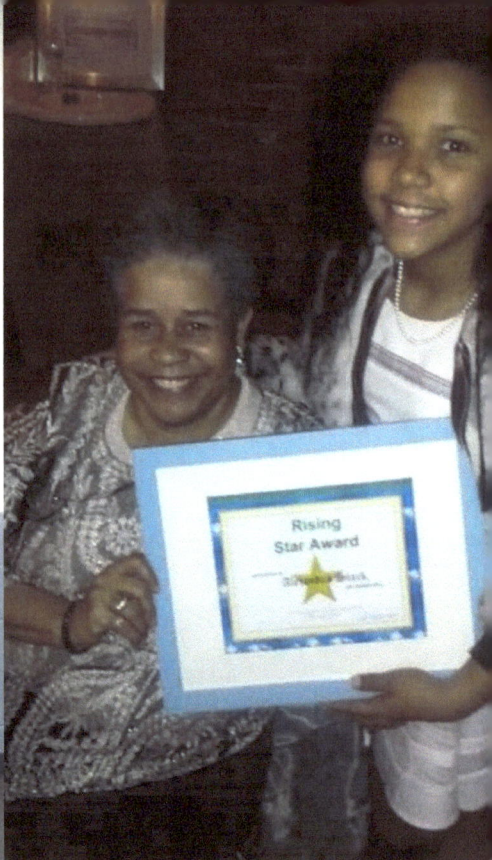

Thanks to Mr. James Stocks and Mrs. Corlis Hudson-Long, I had the opportunity to see some of the places I read about in the history lessons they taught us. I also got to participate in NAACP events and meet some of the people who protested during the American Civil Rights Movement and people who were about making a change in the present day.

I went on many trips to learn about prominent figures, the majority of them were of relevance during the Civil Rights Movement. I learned a lot of things that I didn't learn in school. In school, we always talked about people like Martin Luther King, Jr and Rosa Parks but while in the NAACP, I learned about groups like the Freedom Riders. The Freedom Riders were a group of White and Black activists who fought for equality. We traveled along the route they took to see the places they made the changes. They did types of protests called "sit ins" where they would sit and stay at counters in segregated restaurants in silence. People would still be incredibly mean and assault them verbally and physically. Although this may not seem like a big deal to us, these people risked their lives to fight for change. Many of them were murdered for simply wanting equal rights.

Even though things now aren't perfect, they are a lot better then they were about 60 years ago because of activists who fought for change. Nowadays, you can sue for racial discrimination and demand people are fired or voted out but back then the Jim Crow laws were designed to keep Black people inequal to basic rights.

As youth council president, I got to meet the last surviving original 13 Freedom Riders Mr. Henry Hank Thomas at an NAACP Freedom Fund Banquet and thanked him for his sacrifice. From 1961, he was arrested over 22 times, lynched, left for dead, but did not give up. He went on to be awarded a Purple Heart after the Vietnam War and became an epic businessman owning multiple businesses. His wife Ms Yvonne was the first Black student to graduate from her college.

I also got to meet Stacey Abrams while she ran for Governor for the State of Georgia and her words encouraged me as a girl in leadership.

Learning was one thing, but to actually visit some sites where these incidents occurred was a different thing. During my time with the NAACP, I went to many different places across the South. I saw Historically Black Colleges and Universities (HBCU's) that were established because Black people were denied an education in White schools. I visited the houses of famous African-Americans who were activists and changemakers in their time. I saw places where Black people were found brutally murdered, saw plantations where they were once enslaved, saw places where police pepper-sprayed protesters and sprayed them with fire hoses and made their dogs attack them.

I visited the home and workplace of Medgar Evers, the NAACP's first field secretary, in Mississippi. I saw the bedrooms of his children, and the tub where they had to hide when people tried to attack their home. I saw the bullet holes that went through his walls at his house and his office window. I saw the driveway where he was shot.

I also saw where the Southern Christian

Leadership Council was formed. I visited the Freedom Riders Museum in Alabama. Being in Atlanta, I often visit the King Center which has the birthplace and final resting place of Dr. Martin Luther King, Jr. and Historic Ebenezer Baptist Church where he became a minister and his mother was later assassinated while she played the organ during church service is adjacent to this site. I have also been to the Lorraine Hotel to see where Dr. King was assassinated.

I also learned about days of service. Where sometimes it's not about a protest but about helping clean up parks or helping seniors. I learned about the importance of voting and getting people registered to vote and offering rides to take them to the polls so their voices could be heard. Voting is very important in communities.

I began learning about the Black Lives Matter movement and why they are active.

I've had the opportunity to travel to many places including Washington, D. C. to see the monuments and museums there, and to many sites in Florida, Georgia, Carolina and the Caribbean to learn the history of the African diaspora in the Americas.

Because I am also an actress and future director/producer, I am homeschooled. That gave me and my mom the opportunity to create my curriculum which includes a lot more African, Caribbean and African-American history. Telling Black culture stories is important to me which is why I still value my role playing young Alicia in Maggie Bush's 'Mixed Emotions' along with Jossie Harris Thacker who showed me that it is okay to identify and embrace my AfroLatina identity.

mixedemotions.tv Happy birthday to @alejandrastack
one of our little babies and stars from
@mixedemotions.tv
Love you AfroLatina ✨✨✨

Meeting people like Alima Albari of Shoot Films Not Guns and participating in the launches allowed me to embrace my love for the film industry and activism. I learned the importance of PSAs (public service announcements) and showed that film can be an amazing tool in activism, whether it is a documentary or a short film.

That project also allowed me to meet former

Youth activists like Clifton Kinnie who went from being a kid activist to starting a nonprofit and using his expertise from what he learned over the years to get the message out. He was inspired to do something after the Michael Brown case in Ferguson Missouri.

Being surrounded by peers and friends like Taylor Richardson who is passionate about STEM education, helping less fortunate and civil rights reminds me that I don't have to pick just one thing to speak about. But whatever I feel resonates with me. It's important to have people in your circle who are your age so you know you can support each other and you are not alone in your cause.

I'm happy to be a part of the Change 4 Hope homeschool hub with Deetra Poindexter who founded the group to give homeschoolers the chance see Black history, meet diverse business owners and visit HBCUs. We also do lots of volunteering and we even helped folks who survived Hurricane Dorian in the Bahamas, where my family is from.

Despite all the lessons I learned and places I had gone, all the peaceful parades I attended, I never thought I would find myself witnessing a protest that would be violent but in the summer of 2020.

That was the summer several Black people were killed by police including Breonna Taylor and George Floyd. When I heard they were going to protest in Atlanta, I asked my mom if I could attend. Initially, she said no. Later she came into my room and asked me what I knew about their deaths, Black Lives Matter, the NAACP and police brutality. Because she likes to make me write things, she told me to write an essay on the subject.

I really didn't feel like writing but I wanted to prove to her I knew. Later, I told her all that I knew and even told her about an Afro-Latino reporter at CNN who was arrested for doing his job covering the protests and I was aware of the risks. She agreed to take me, reminding me that there is a difference between protesting and rioting. She also warned me that things could get violent, that we were going to observe and not provoke anyone. We packed kits that included water, gauze pads, notepads and pens, identification and containers of milk and cream just in case we were near pepper spray since that's what the Civil Rights Movement protesters used when their eyes got burned.

We went to Centennial Olympic Park and the CNN center and I watched in shock as a place I loved hanging out looked like a war zone as protestors were everywhere chanting, journalists were documenting and armed officers were everywhere. Suddenly, we heard a loud crack and saw that people were breaking windows and destroying property. I wanted to take video and pictures but was reminded not to get too close and to remember the lessons about peaceful protesting not violent rioting. I took out my phone and documented as much as I could. I have one of the only videos that showed the officers coming down to a CNN entrance holding their weapons as people began breaking windows..

Then there was a loud pop and smoke everywhere as they threw tear gas into the crowds. I
began choking and my throat started burning
and my eyes became watery. My mom took me
a safe distance away and even though I wanted to go back, she reminded me that a good
journalist documents the story and avoids being a part of the story. Still, I ended up getting

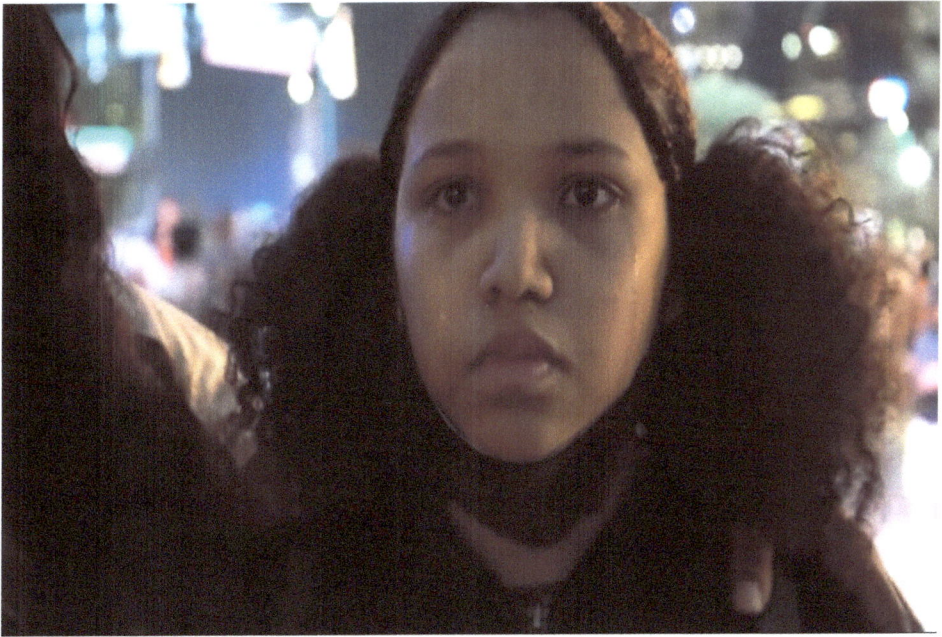

In These Streets is based out of the streets of Atlanta.
Former Jr NAACP President Alejandra gives emotional
interview
#inthesestreets #CNN #Protest #Atlanta
#BLM #GeorgeFloyd #aubreyahmad #breonnataylor
Protestor speaks on injustices, BLM and the time to change
is now!

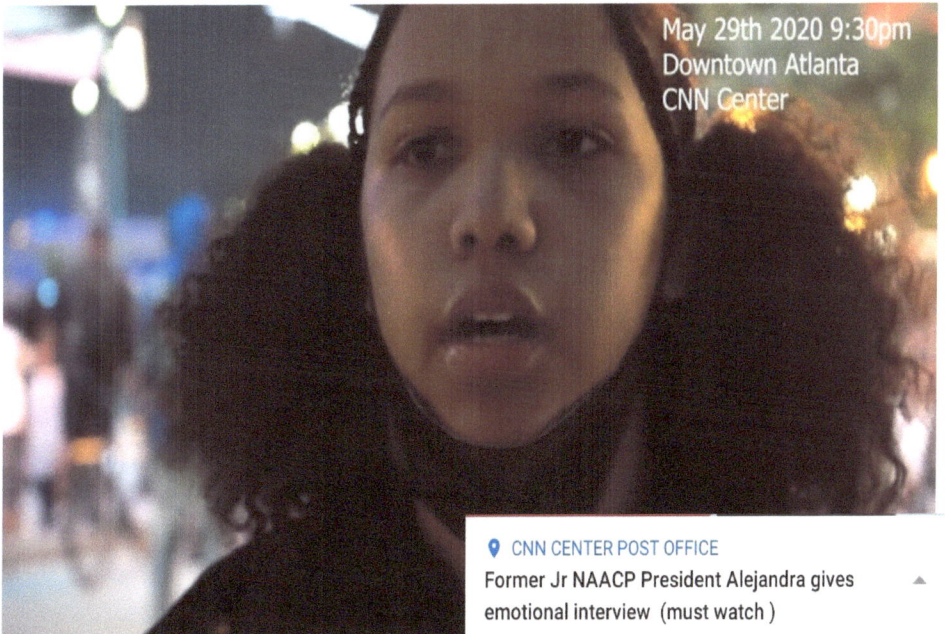

May 29th 2020 9:30pm
Downtown Atlanta
CNN Center

📍 CNN CENTER POST OFFICE
Former Jr NAACP President Alejandra gives
emotional interview (must watch)

interviewed when someone recognized me and I broke into tears when asked how I felt about the evening. It was just overwhelming because I felt that after centuries of systematic oppression, people were still being brutalized. As things got a bit more active, my mom decided it was best we go home.

My videos and photos were shared all over social media and people began inviting me to speak on talk shows, the news and at youth events.

When I got home, I watched the protests live while going through social media to figure out how I could bring awareness to the situation and that young people have voices in the matter too because so many kids were victims or saw the their loved ones killed.

It was Clara McLaughlin, the first Black woman to own a tv station in the USA who gave me

my first newspaper space to tell stories at age 9. I met her at a Gullah Geechee festival and my mom worked with her media house. She gave me a Black History trivia game and told my to always tell our stories.

This is why I wrote this book. To encourage you to find something you are passionate about to activate your inner activist. This is my story. Begin yours.

BLACK LIVES MATTER 101
GUEST SPEAKER
Alejandra Sta
YOUNG ACTIVIST and
COMMUNITY LEADER

BLACK *Class*

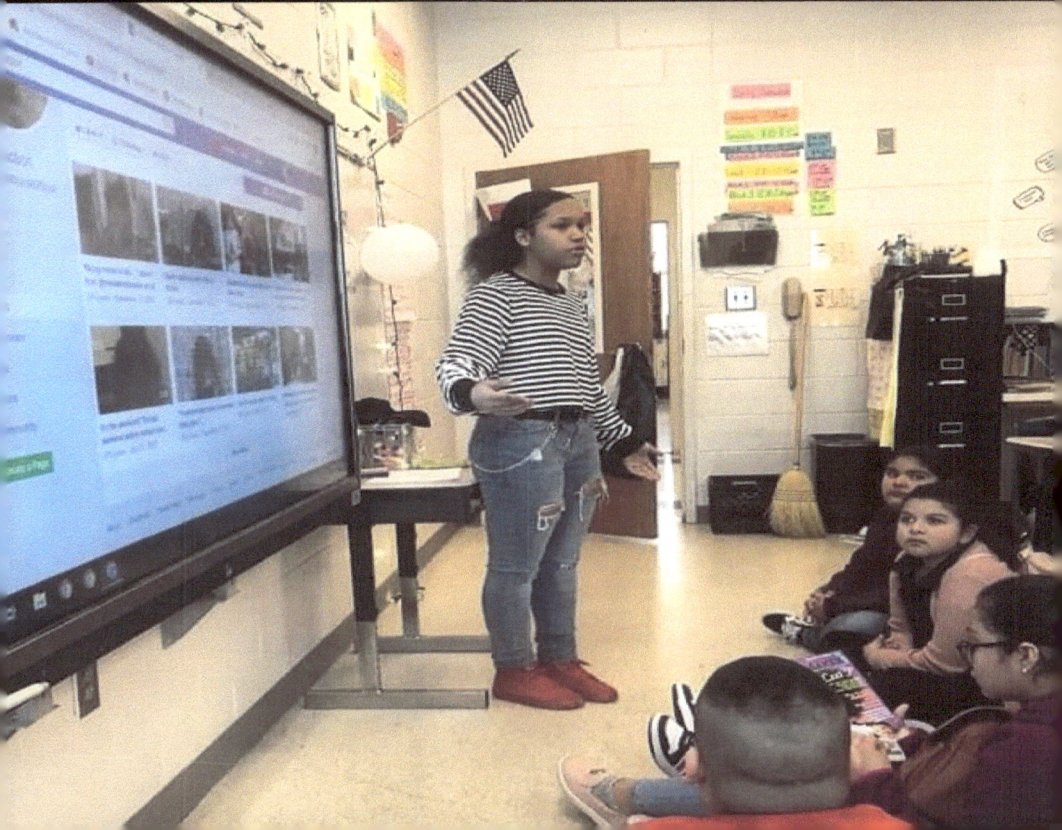

What is an activist?

According to the dictionary, an activist is "a person who campaigns to bring about political or social change." This basically means that an activist is someone who works to support a cause that is important to them.

Do I have to be an activist for the same cause you want to highlight?

No you don't. There are amazing kids and teens who are activists for the environment, for animals, for education, for human rights, for gender equality, for disability rights or whatever they relate to or what they think they are most passionate about. Write down three things you are passionate about and pick one. You can be an activist of multiple things.

What are five things a kid should do when they are out protesting?

Make sure you go with a parent or trusted adult and stay close to them at all times

Wear sensible clothing like jeans and tennis shoes not sandals just in case you have to run

Bring a small bag for things like water, hand sanitizer, and milk.

Try not to get in the middle of big rowdy crowds, just in case. You don't want to get trampled.

Keep your eyes open. Make sure you're aware of your surroundings at all times. If you see someone that looks like they may be up to no good, tell whoever you're with and move away. Better safe than sorry. And do not get into other people's personal space or provoke others. Also have an escape plan in advance.

How can a kid tell their parents they want to be an activist?

The best way to tell your parents you want to be an activist is having a plan and doing research on it. Anyone can say they want to do something but not everyone can come up with reasons why they want to do it. Activism isn't just a trend. Make sure it's something you're really passionate about. Collect information about whatever it is you want to do so that when you present it to your parents they can see that you're really serious about it. Why are you passionate about your cause?

_____

_____

_____

_____

_____

_____

_____

_____

Some parents may not want to take their kids to be a part of activism because the protests turn violent. What's the difference between a protest and a riot?

There's a big difference between a protest and a riot. In basic terms, a protest is a group of people peacefully trying to get their point across. All protests are pre-organized meaning everyone involved is aware of what they're protesting. A riot is when people destroy property and become rowdy and violent. Riots can include things like looting and arson, and even bodily harm.

How can one become educated on a cause and what are some important things to remember?

You can always research online or find information in books. If you know someone who is an activist, don't be afraid to ask for wisdom and knowledge. You should remember to not force your opinions on others and don't make fun of someone for not knowing something, you're supposed to share knowledge with others. Always remember change doesn't come immediately, don't be discouraged, and continue to prevail.

In most protests, people have creative signs to let others know what they are protesting about. Grab some markers or crayons and make your own protest sign.

What are five things a kid can do if they are not allowed to go to a protest?

Inform others. Knowledge and education is the most powerful thing in the world.

Make sure to educate others and to be respectful if they don't agree with your view of things.

Make social media posts to let people know you stand in solidarity.

If you have any extra birthday money or money from chores you can ask your parents to donate it to your cause.

Ask your parents if you could host your own meeting or protest with friends.

Reshare content already out there from the organization.

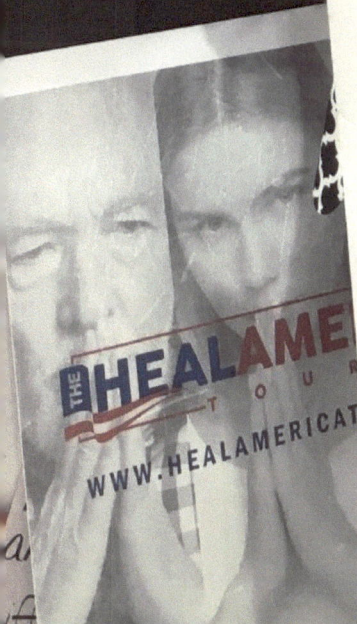

COMMUNITY

Stack wins Rising Star Award   Clark earns Lifetime Achievem

Jessica Gallagher/Times-Georgian

NAACP Youth Council President Alejandra Stack, 11, was presented the MLK Rising Star Award on Saturday night during the Martin Luther King Holiday Weekend Celebration Gala at Carrollton's historic train depot on Bradley Street. Alejandra is a Carrollton Junior High honors student who was awarded for her role with the youth council and her entrepreneurial efforts. Michelle Lewis presented the award. Alejandra is the daughter of Arthia Nixon.

Ora Belle Clark was pr
night for her contribu
tor Felix Moten pres
Celebration Gala a

ABOUT THE AUTHOR

Alejandra Stack was born in 2005 to a Bahamian mother and Spanish Canadian father. She spent her early childhood in Eleuthera, Bahamas , Montreal, Canada and Atlanta, Georgia. She was exposed to newsrooms and the arts at an early age through her mother and met many influential figures.

She began her first business at age four and had a newspaper column in two states by age nine. Allie has also appeared in several projects including *Mixed Emotions, The Walking Dead, Tyler Perry's Ruthless, Stephen King's Dr. Sleep, R.L. Stein's Fear Street 2,* and *Little.*

To make time for her projects and to have a curriculum tailored for her interests and future goals, Allie began homeschooling in middle school.

Allie has won numerous awards including an Martin Luther King Jr Rising Star Award and has received city, state, national and international recognitions.

She enjoys the arts, particularly drama and painting. She also likes listening to music, travelling, horseback riding, enjoying Caribbean culture, and learning more about the film industry and media.

www.ingramcontent.com/pod-product-compliance
Lightning Source LLC
LaVergne TN
LVHW010023070426
835508LV00001B/19